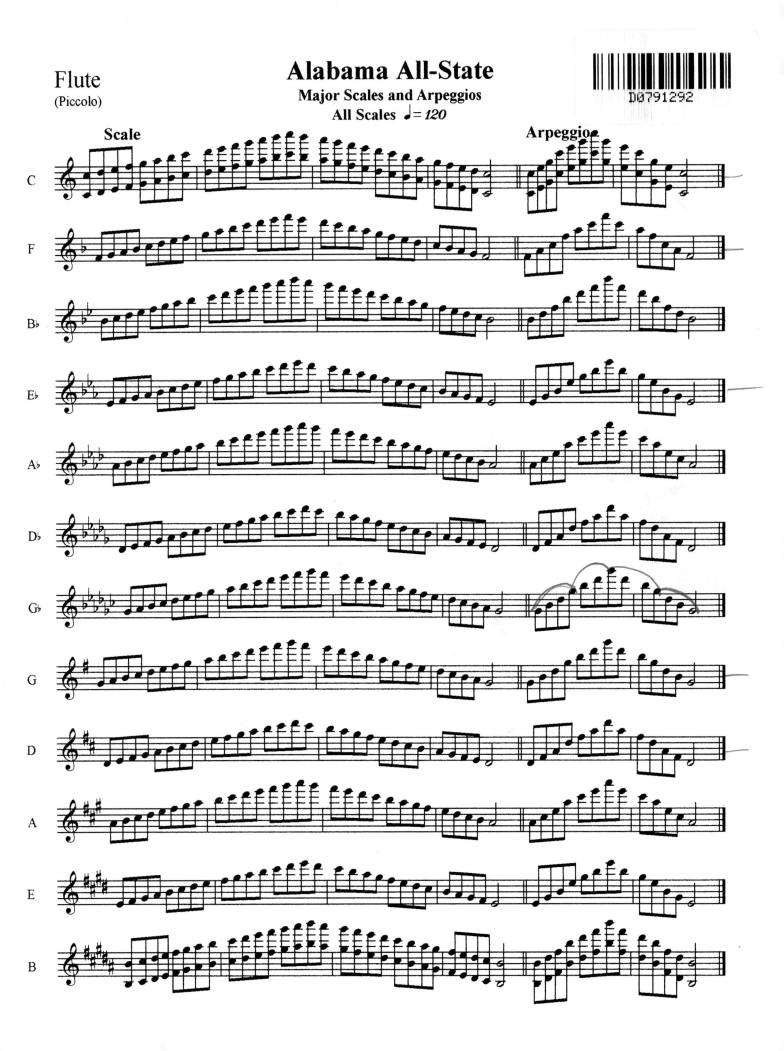

THRILLER

Recorded by MICHAEL JACKSON

PART 1
Flute

Words and Music by
ROD TEMPERTON
Arranged by JOHNNIE VINSON

Pomp and Circumstance Marches

FLUTE

Edward Elgar
Arr. by Mark Williams

1.	**ajouter**	to add	
2.	**bouillir**	to boil	
3.	**c'est compliqué**	it's complicated	
4.	**c'est facile de faire...?**	is it easy to make...?	
5.	**c'est très simple**	it's very simple	
6.	**comment est-ce qu'on fait...**	how do you make...?	
7.	**couper**	to cut	
8.	**faire cuire**	to bake, to cook	
9.	**Il te faut autre chose?**	Do you need anything else?	
10.	**il y a...**	there is/ there are...	
11.	**je suis trop occupé(e)**	i'm too busy.	
12.	**l' huile**	oil	
13.	**l'abricot**	apricot	
14.	**l'ail**	garlic	
15.	**l'aubergine**	eggplant	
16.	**l'huile d'olive**	olive oil	
17.	**l'oignon**	onion	
18.	**la banane**	banana	
19.	**la carotte**	carrot	
20.	**la cerise**	cherry	
21.	**la courgette**	zucchini	
22.	**la cuisinière**	stove	
23.	**la farine**	flour	
24.	**la fraise**	strawberry	
25.	**la framboise**	raspberry	
26.	**la laitue**	lettuce	
27.	**la pastèque**	watermelon	
28.	**la pêche**	peach	
29.	**la poire**	pear	
30.	**la pomme**	apple	
31.	**la pomme de terre**	potato	
32.	**la tomate**	tomato	
33.	**le brocoli**	broccoli	
34.	**le champignon**	mushroom	
35.	**le four**	oven	
36.	**le melon**	melon	
37.	**le poivron**	bell pepper	
39.	**les épices**	spices	
40.	**les haricots verts**	green beans	
41.	**les petits pois**	peas	
42.	**mélanger**	to mix	
43.	**n'oublie pas...**	don't forget...	
44.	**non, je regrette mais...**	no, i am sorry but....	
45.	**oui, j'y vais tout de suite**	yes, i'll go there right away	
46.	**qu'est-ce qu'il y a dans..?**	what's in...?	
47.	**rapporte (- moi)**	bring (me)...	
48.	**tu me rapportes...?**	can you bring me...?	
49.	**Tu n'as besoin de rien d'autre?**	Do you need anything else?	
50.	**tu veux bien...?**	can you/ would you mind...?	
51.	**une cuillerée à café**	teaspoon	
52.	**une cuillerée à soupe**	tablespoon	
53.	**une tasse de...**	a cup of...	

1.	**ajouter**	to add		
2.	**bouillir**	to boil		
3.	**c'est compliqué**	it's complicated		
4.	**c'est facile de faire...?**	is it easy to make...?		
5.	**c'est très simple**	it's very simple		
6.	**comment est-ce qu'on fait...**	how do you make...?		
7.	**couper**	to cut		
8.	**faire cuire**	to bake, to cook		
9.	**Il te faut autre chose?**	Do you need anything else?		
10.	**il y a...**	there is/ there are...		
11.	**je suis trop occupé(e)**	i'm too busy.		
12.	**l' huile**	oil		
13.	**l'abricot**	apricot		
14.	**l'ail**	garlic		
15.	**l'aubergine**	eggplant		
16.	**l'huile d'olive**	olive oil		
17.	**l'oignon**	onion		
18.	**la banane**	banana		
19.	**la carotte**	carrot		
20.	**la cerise**	cherry		
21.	**la courgette**	zucchini		
22.	**la cuisinière**	stove		
23.	**la farine**	flour		
24.	**la fraise**	strawberry		
25.	**la framboise**	raspberry		
26.	**la laitue**	lettuce		
27.	**la pastèque**	watermelon		
28.	**la pêche**	peach		
29.	**la poire**	pear		
30.	**la pomme**	apple		
31.	**la pomme de terre**	potato		
32.	**la tomate**	tomato		
33.	**le brocoli**	broccoli		
34.	**le champignon**	mushroom		
35.	**le four**	oven		
36.	**le melon**	melon		
37.	**le poivron**	bell pepper		

39.	**les épices**	spices
40.	**les haricots verts**	green beans
41.	**les petits pois**	peas
42.	**mélanger**	to mix
43.	**n'oublie pas...**	don't forget...
44.	**non, je regrette mais...**	no, i am sorry but....
45.	**oui, j'y vais tout de suite**	yes, i'll go there right away
46.	**qu'est-ce qu'il y a dans..?**	what's in...?
47.	**rapporte (- moi)**	bring (me)...
48.	**tu me rapportes...?**	can you bring me...?
49.	**Tu n'as besoin de rien d'autre?**	Do you need anything else?
50.	**tu veux bien...?**	can you/ would you mind...?
51.	**une cuillerée à café**	teaspoon
52.	**une cuillerée à soupe**	tablespoon
53.	**une tasse de...**	a cup of...

AGENDA

Friday, October 25, 2013	
6:00 pm-8:00 pm	CONFERENCE REGISTRATION
9:00 pm-10:30 pm	Zumba Dance and Photo Scavenger Hunt
11:00 pm-6:00 am	CURFEW (Everyone in Own Assigned Rooms)
Saturday, October 26, 2013	
8:00am	LYNBROOK CHAPTER BREAKFAST ☺ We will provide an awesome breakfast for you. Bagels, juice, etc. Meeting place TBA.
9:00 am-9:30 am	OFFICER WORKSHOPS
9:00 am-9:45 am	LEADERSHIP SESSION I
10:00 am-11:10 am	OPENING SESSION Keynote: Ro Khanna, former Undersecretary of Commerce, Obama Administration
11:15 am-12:00 pm	LEADERSHIP SESSION II
12:00 pm-1:20 pm	LUNCH (on your own)
1:30 pm-2:15 pm	LEADERSHIP SESSION III
2:25 pm-3:10 pm	LEADERSHIP SESSION IV
3:10 pm-3:25 pm	BREAK
3:25 pm-4:10 pm	LEADERSHIP SESSION V
4:20 pm-5:05 pm	LEADERSHIP SESSION VI
5:10 pm	TURN IN CONFERENCE EVALUATION FORMS TO AMIT You must attend six workshops to earn Honors.
6:30pm	LYNBROOK CHAPTER DINNER ☺ Food/drinks/dessert will be provided, and we will be playing fun games such as Taboo and Business Mafia. Meeting place TBA.
8:30 pm-11:00 pm	MARCH OF DIMES BLUE JEANS FOR BABIES DANCE The dance is a fundraiser for March of Dimes and your donation of $2 will entitle you to dress in casual attire. *Please Note: This dance is part of the conference, and you must conduct yourself appropriately. If you are being inappropriate in your dance style you will be excused from the dance. Advisers and chaperones will be supervising the dance.*
11:30 pm-6:00 am	CURFEW (Everyone in Own Assigned Rooms)
Sunday, October 27, 2013	

Name *Bahaar Bhatia*

Flute

Foundations for Superior Performance
Warm-Ups and Technique for Band
by Richard Williams and Jeff King

A comprehensive and sequential book of warm-ups, scales, technical patterns, chord studies, tuning exercises, and chorales for concert band.

Designed to organize the daily rehearsal and advance the performance level of the ensemble.

Practical and efficient exercises in all twelve major keys developed in the classroom.

Table of Contents

Section 1: Warm-Ups
- Concert F Around the Band 2
- Articulation Exercises 3
- Long Tones 4-5
- Warm-Up Sets 1 through 4 6-9

Section 2: Technique
Major and minor scales, mini-scales, scale patterns, scales in thirds, intervals, triads, and chord studies.
- Concert B♭ 10-11
- Concert F 12-13
- Concert C 14-15
- Concert G 16-17
- Concert D 18
- Concert A 19
- Concert E 20
- Concert B 21
- Concert G♭ 22-23
- Concert D♭ 24-25
- Concert A♭ 26-27
- Concert E♭ 28-29

Section 3: Chorales and Tuning Exercises
Interval tuning, chord tuning, and chorales
- Concert B♭ 30-31
- Concert F 32-33
- Concert E♭ 34-35
- Concert C 36
- Concert c minor 37
- Concert G 38
- Concert g minor 39
- Concert A♭ 40

Appendix:
- Circle of Fifths 41
- One Octave Scales and Arpeggios 42
- Full Range Scales 44
- Chromatic Scales 46
- Major Arpeggios and Inversions 48

ISBN 0-8497-7004-1

©1997 **Neil A. Kjos Music Company**, 4380 Jutland Drive, San Diego, California 92117
International copyright secured. All rights reserved. Printed in U.S.A.

kjos Neil A. Kjos Music Company • *Publisher*

Concert F Around The Band

Each instrument will play concert F in their middle register. The flute is a concert pitch instrument, there is no transposition for flute.

Copy the note in measure one into measure two.

Your director will divide the band into various sections or groups for the listening drill Concert F Around The Band.

Once the instruments have been placed into groups, write the name of the instrument(s) in the appropriate box below (every box may not be used).

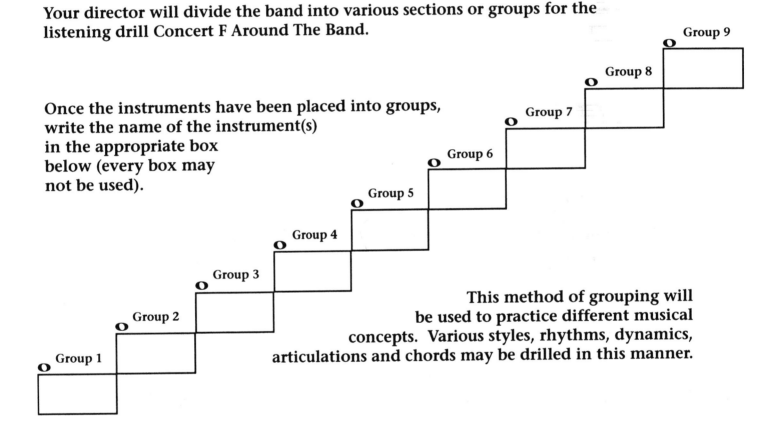

This method of grouping will be used to practice different musical concepts. Various styles, rhythms, dynamics, articulations and chords may be drilled in this manner.

As you play the exercise, keep the following concepts in mind:

- match the primary parts of each note (attack-sustain-release)

- work for a smooth shape to each note (no bumps in the sound)

- hand off tenuto notes (full value) without creating "holes" between the attacks

- match intonation, intensity, volume, tone quality, and the "body of sound"

- be aware of the different colors (timbres) of the instrument groups and their location in the room

- listen from the bottom groups and balance low-middle-high

Articulation Exercises

Articulations: A Study in Styles

Four connected quarter-notes (tenuto). The sound of one note "touches" the next note.

Four quarter-notes in "lifted" style. The attack is the same as tenuto, but the end of the note is tapered.

Four quarter-notes "lifted and short" (staccato). Separated and detached (half full value).

Eighth-notes in connected style.

Eighth-notes in lifted and short style.

Eighth-note triplets in connected style.

Eighth-note triplets in a detached style (bounced).

Sixteenth-notes in a connected style.

Articulation Exercise on Concert F

* opt. ending on whole note

Long Tones

Concert F Descending

Long Tone 1

Long Tone 2

Long Tone 3

3a *intervals of a minor 2nd*   *intervals of a major 2nd*

intervals of a minor 3rd   *intervals of a major 3rd*

intervals of a perfect 4th   *intervals of an augmented 4th*

intervals of a perfect 5th

3b *intervals of a minor 2nd*   *intervals of a major 2nd*   *intervals of a minor 3rd*

intervals of a major 3rd   *intervals of a perfect 4th*   *intervals of an augmented 4th*

Warm-Up Set 1

Option 1 (unison "lip slur" with brass)

Option 2 (unison harmonic study with brass)

○ indicate a note produced as a harmonic

◆ indicate the fingered note

Options 3, 4, & 5 (technical patterns with brass lip slurs)

Articulation Patterns:

Warm-Up Set 2

Option 1 (unison "lip slur" with brass)

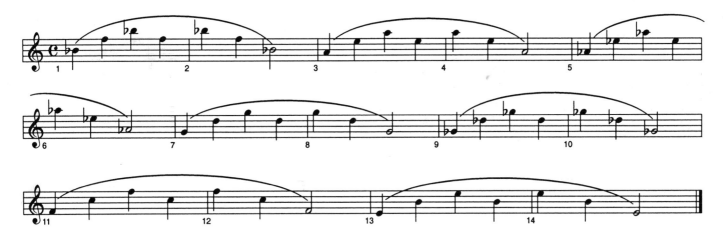

Option 2 (unison harmonic study with brass)

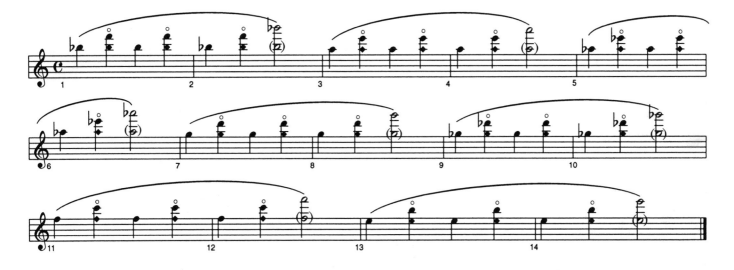

Options 3, 4, & 5 (technical patterns with brass lip slurs)

Articulation Patterns:

Warm-Up Set 3

Option 1 (unison "lip slur" with brass)

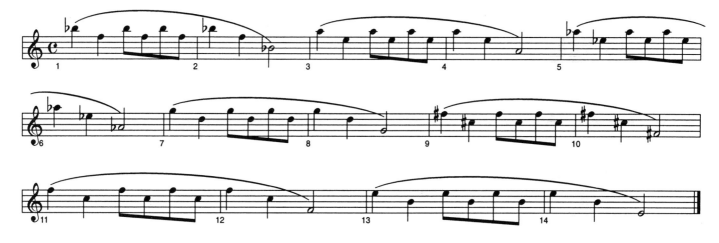

Option 2 (unison harmonic study with brass)

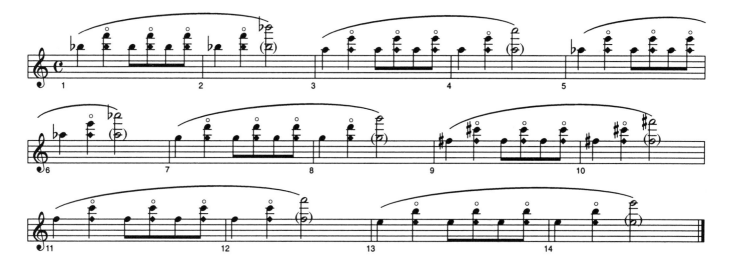

Options 3, 4, & 5 (technical patterns with brass lip slurs)

Warm-Up Set 4

Option 1 (unison "lip slur" with brass)

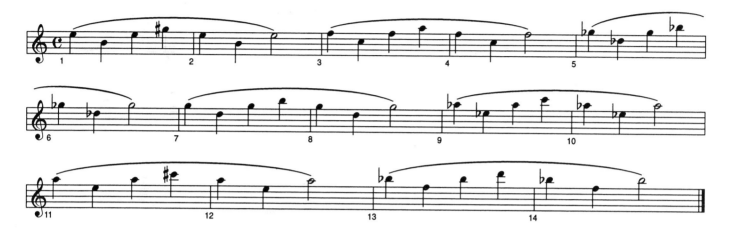

Option 2 (unison harmonic study with brass)

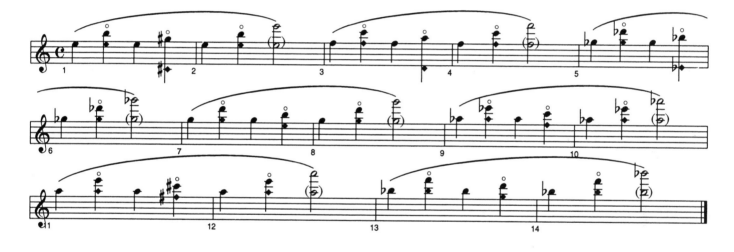

Options 3, 4, & 5 (technical patterns with brass lip slurs)

Articulation Patterns:

Technical Exercises in the Key of B♭

Major Scale

Natural Minor

Harmonic Minor

Melodic Minor

Mini-Scale & Tonic Arpeggio

Scale Pattern 1 *articulations:*

Scale Pattern 2*

Scale in Thirds*

Interval Study

Triads of the B♭ Scale

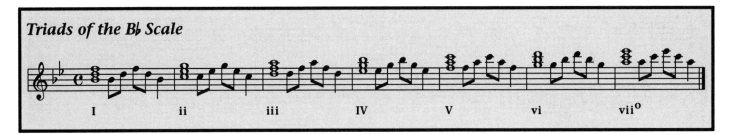

Chord Study 1*

Chord Study 2 - *articulations:*

Technical Exercises in the Key of F

Major Scale

Natural Minor

Harmonic Minor

Melodic Minor

Mini-Scale & Tonic Arpeggio

(also practice 8va w/cue note)

Scale Pattern 1 *articulations:*

Scale Pattern 2*

Scale in Thirds*

Interval Study

Triads of the F Scale

I   ii   iii   IV   V   vi   vii°

Chord Study 1*

Chord Study 2 - articulations:

Technical Exercises in the Key of C

Major Scale

Natural Minor

Harmonic Minor

Melodic Minor

Mini-Scale & Tonic Arpeggio

(also practice 8vb)

Scale Pattern 1 **articulations:*

Scale Pattern 2*

Scale in Thirds*

(also practice 8va w/♩ option)

Interval Study

Triads of the C Scale

I ii iii IV V vi vii°

Chord Study 1*

Chord Study 2 - articulations:

Technical Exercises in the Key of G

Major Scale

Natural Minor

Harmonic Minor

Melodic Minor

Mini-Scale & Tonic Arpeggio

Scale Pattern 1 *articulations:

Scale Pattern 2*

Scale in Thirds*

Interval Study

Triads of the G Scale

I   ii   iii   IV   V   vi   vii°

Chord Study 1*

Chord Study 2 - *articulations:*

Technical Exercises in the Key of D

Major Scale

Natural Minor

Harmonic Minor

Melodic Minor

Mini-Scale & Tonic Arpeggio

(also practice 8va w/cue note)

Scale in Thirds - articulations:

Technical Exercises in the Key of A

Major Scale

Natural Minor

Harmonic Minor

Melodic Minor

Mini-Scale & Tonic Arpeggio

Scale in Thirds - *articulations:*

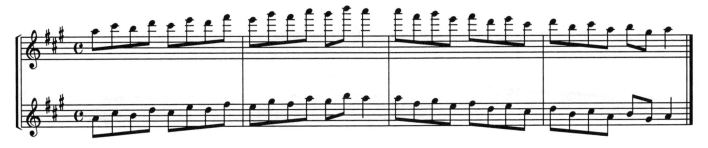

Technical Exercises in the Key of E

Major Scale

Natural Minor

Harmonic Minor

Melodic Minor

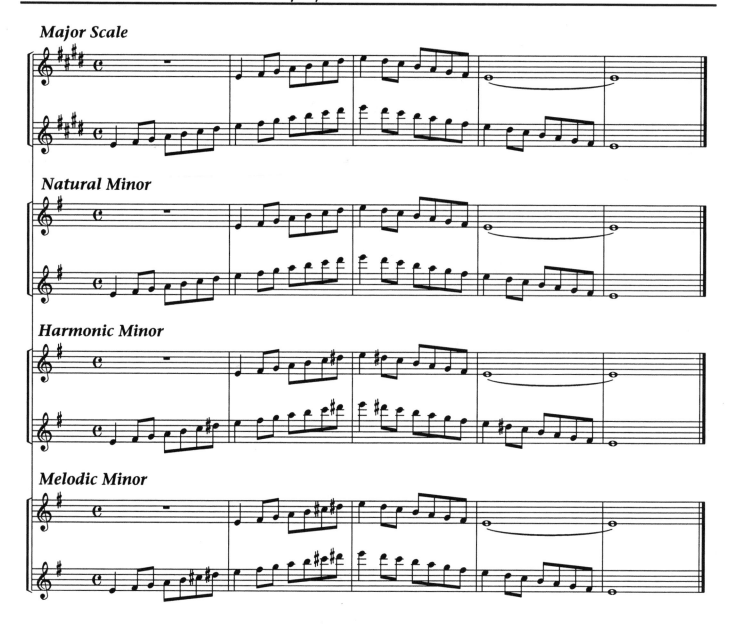

Mini-Scale & Tonic Arpeggio

(also practice 8va w/cue note)

Scale in Thirds - *articulations:*

Technical Exercises in the Key of B

Major Scale

Natural Minor

Harmonic Minor

Melodic Minor

Mini-Scale & Tonic Arpeggio

Scale in Thirds - articulations:

Technical Exercises in the Key of G♭

Major Scale

Natural Minor

Harmonic Minor

Melodic Minor

Mini-Scale & Tonic Arpeggio

Scale Pattern 1 *articulations:*

Scale Pattern 2*

Scale in Thirds*

Interval Study

Triads of the G♭ Scale

I   ii   iii   IV   V   vi   vii°

Chord Study 1*

Chord Study 2 - articulations:

Technical Exercises in the Key of D♭

Major Scale

Natural Minor

Harmonic Minor

Melodic Minor

Mini-Scale & Tonic Arpeggio

(also practice 8va w/cue note)

Scale Pattern 1 *articulations:

(also practice 8va)

Scale Pattern 2*

(also practice 8va)

Scale in Thirds*

Interval Study

Triads of the D♭ Scale

I   ii   iii   IV   V   vi   vii°

Chord Study 1*

Chord Study 2 - articulations:

Technical Exercises in the Key of A♭

Major Scale

Natural Minor

Harmonic Minor

Melodic Minor

Mini-Scale & Tonic Arpeggio

Scale Pattern 1 **articulations:*

Scale Pattern 2*

Scale in Thirds*

Interval Study

Triads of the A♭ Scale

I   ii   iii   IV   V   vi   vii°

Chord Study 1*

Chord Study 2 - articulations:

Technical Exercises in the Key of E♭

Major Scale

Natural Minor

Harmonic Minor

Melodic Minor

Mini-Scale & Tonic Arpeggio

(also practice 8va w/cue note)

Scale Pattern 1 **articulations:*

(also practice 8va)

Scale Pattern 2*

(also practice 8va)

Scale in Thirds*

Interval Study

Triads of the E♭ Scale

I   ii   iii   IV   V   vi   vii°

Chord Study 1*

Chord Study 2 - articulations:

Chorales & Tuning Exercises in B♭

Interval Tuning

1 Intervals from tonic (major 3rd, perfect 4th, perfect 5th)

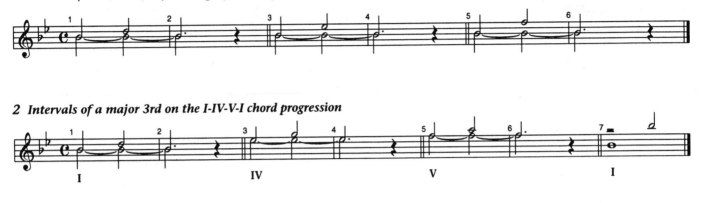

2 Intervals of a major 3rd on the I-IV-V-I chord progression

3 Intervals of a perfect 5th on the I-IV-V-I chord progression

Chord Tuning

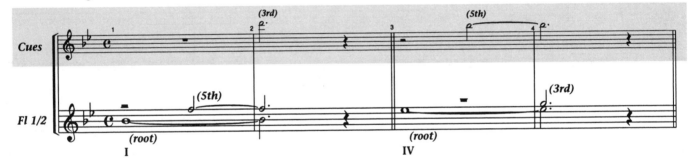

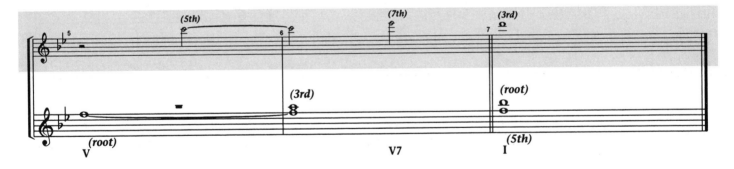

Chorale 1 (full band)

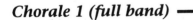

Chorale 2 (full band)

Chorale Melody on Chester

Chester (full band)

Chorales & Tuning Exercises in F

Interval Tuning

1 Intervals from tonic (major 3rd, perfect 4th, perfect 5th)

2 Intervals of a major 3rd on the I-IV-V-I chord progression

3 Intervals of a perfect 5th on the I-IV-V-I chord progression

Chord Tuning

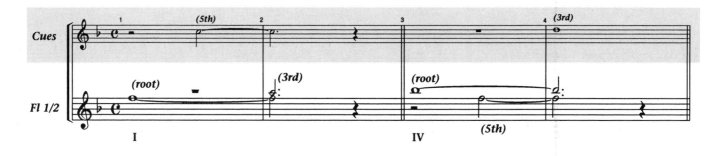

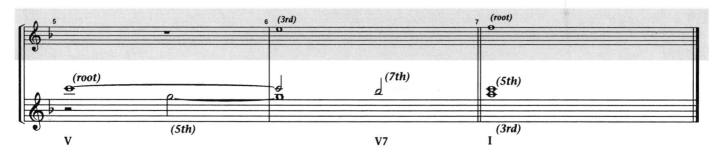

Chorale 3 (full band)

Chorale 4 (full band)

Chorale Melody on Bach 95

Bach 95 (full band)

Chorales & Tuning Exercises in E♭

Interval Tuning

1 Intervals from tonic (major 3rd, perfect 4th, perfect 5th)

2 Intervals of a major 3rd on the I-IV-V-I chord progression

3 Intervals of a perfect 5th on the I-IV-V-I chord progression

Chord Tuning

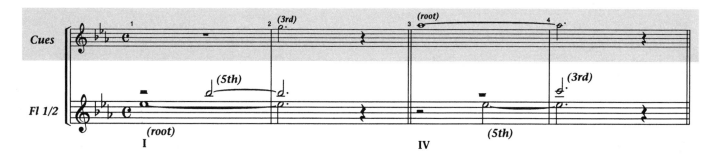

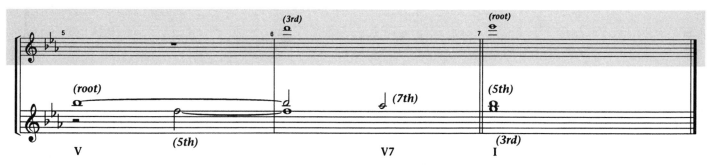

Chorale 5 (full band)

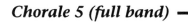

Chorale 6 (full band)

Chorale Melody on America

America (full band)

Chorale & Tuning Exercises in C

Interval Tuning

1 Intervals from tonic (major 3rd, perfect 4th, perfect 5th)

Chord Tuning

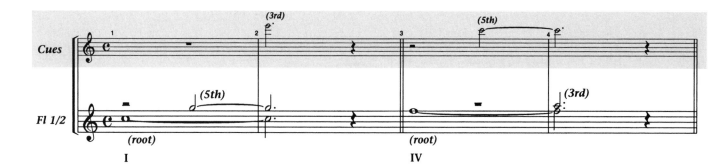

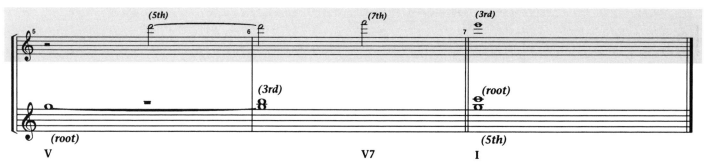

Air (full band)

Chorale & Tuning Exercises in c minor

Interval Tuning

1 *Intervals from tonic (minor 3rd, perfect 4th, perfect 5th)*

Chord Tuning

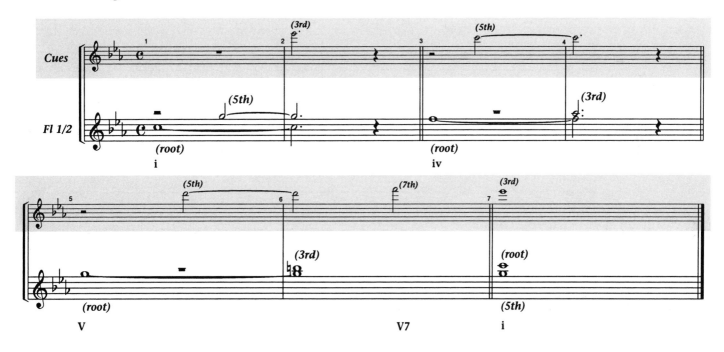

Greensleeves (full band)

Chorale & Tuning Exercises in G

Interval Tuning

1 *Intervals from tonic (major 3rd, perfect 4th, perfect 5th)*

Chord Tuning

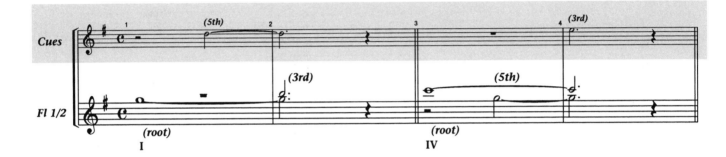

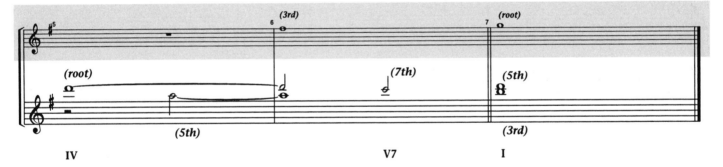

Pavane (full band)

Chorale & Tuning Exercises in g minor

Interval Tuning

1 Intervals from tonic (minor 3rd, perfect 4th, perfect 5th)

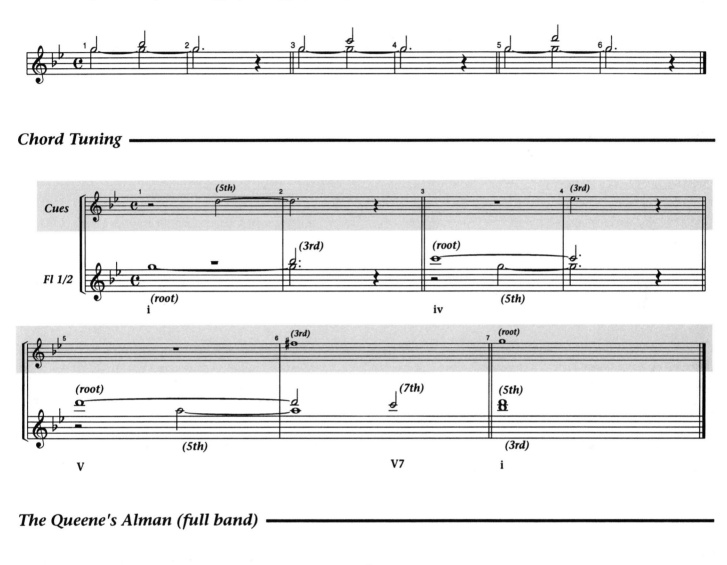

Chord Tuning

The Queene's Alman (full band)

Chorale & Tuning Exercises in A♭

Interval Tuning

1 Intervals from tonic (major 3rd, perfect 4th, perfect 5th)

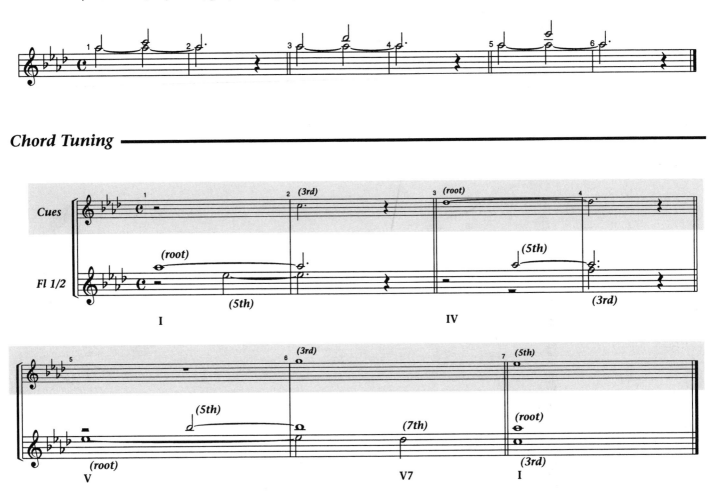

Chord Tuning

All Through the Night (full band)

Appendix

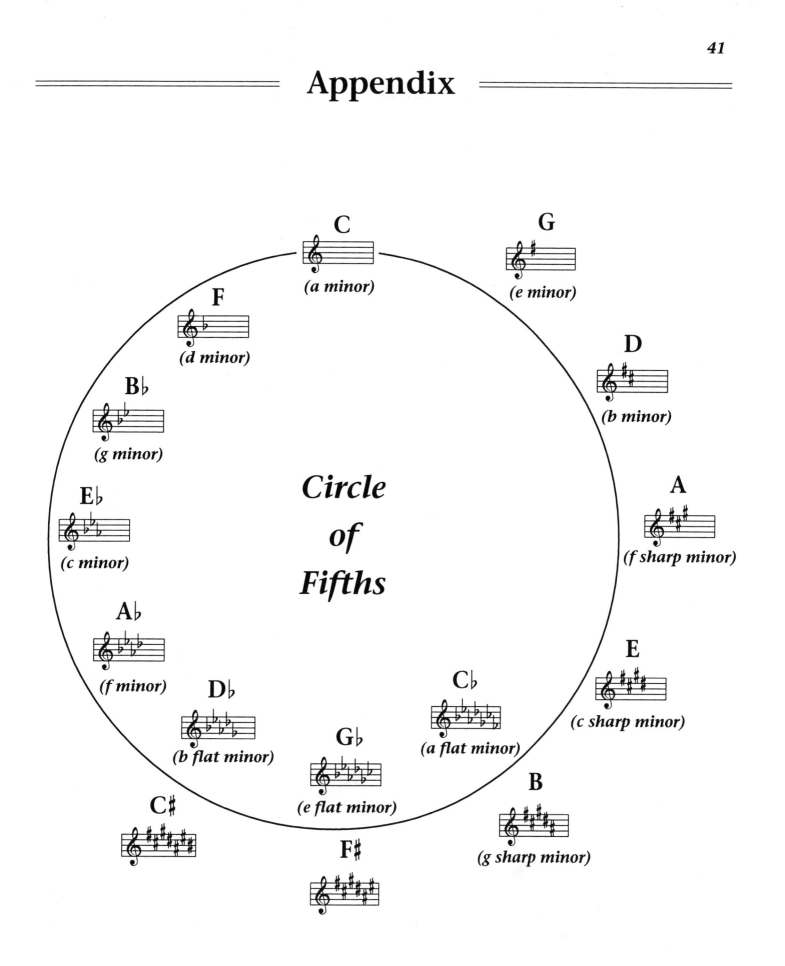

Circle of Fifths

C (a minor)

G (e minor)

F (d minor)

D (b minor)

B♭ (g minor)

A (f sharp minor)

E♭ (c minor)

E (c sharp minor)

A♭ (f minor)

C♭ (a flat minor)

D♭ (b flat minor)

B (g sharp minor)

C♯ (c sharp minor)

G♭ (e flat minor)

F♯

One Octave Scales & Arpeggios

In All Twelve Major Key Signatures

Chromatic Exercises

B♭ Chromatic Scale

F Chromatic Scale

Full Range Scales

In All Twelve Major Key Signatures

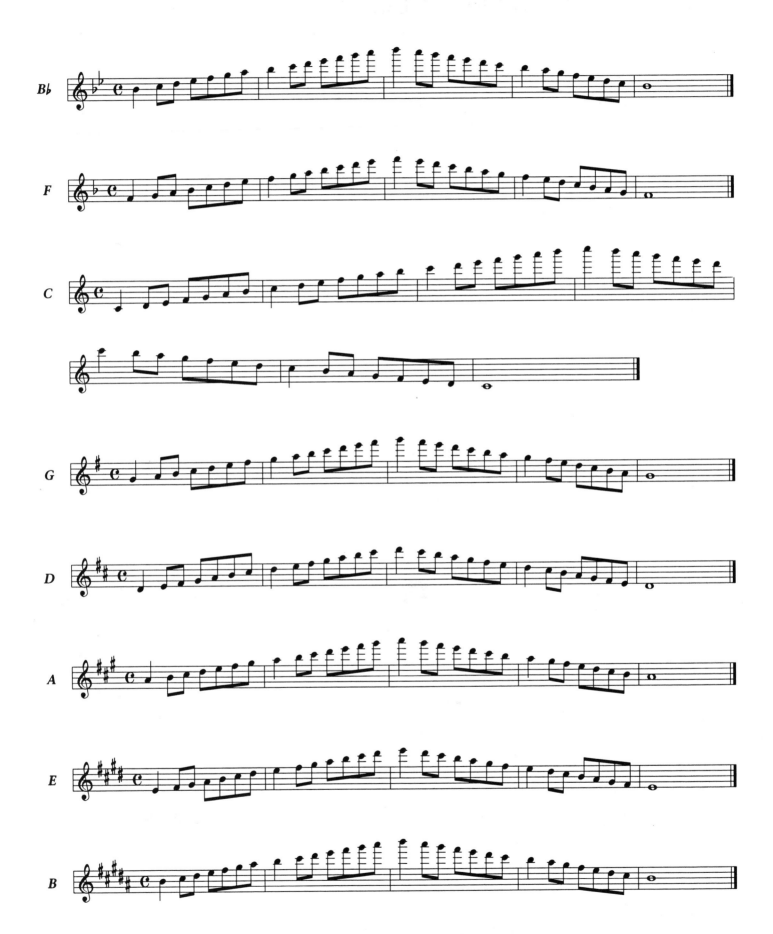

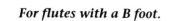

B

F#

G♭

D♭

A♭

E♭

Full Range Chromatic - For Flutes Only

Chromatic Scales

C

(also practice 8va)

Db

D

Eb

E

F